SPEED RACERS

# RACING BMX BIKES

Jane Katirgis and
Ellen C. Labrecque

Enslow Publishing
101 W. 23rd Street
Suite 240
New York, NY 10011
USA
enslow.com

Published in 2018 by Enslow Publishing, LLC.
101 W. 23rd Street, Suite 240, New York, NY 10011



**Library of Congress Cataloging-in-Publication Data**
Names: Katirgis, Jane, author. | Labrecque, Ellen, author.
Title: Racing BMX bikes / Jane Katirgis and Ellen C. Labrecque.
Description: New York : Enslow Publishing, 2018. | Series: Speed racers | Includes bibliographical references and index.
Identifiers: LCCN 2017020412| ISBN 9780766092730 (library bound) | ISBN 9780766094123 (pbk.) | ISBN 9780766094130 (6 pack) Subjects: LCSH: Bicycle motocross—Juvenile literature.
Classification: LCC GV1049.3 .K37 2018 | DDC 796.6/22—dc23
LC record available at https://lccn.loc.gov/2017020412

Printed in the United States of America

**To Our Readers:** We have done our best to make sure all websites in this book were active and appropriate when we went to press. However, the author and the publisher have no control over and assume no liability for the material available on those websites or on any websites they may link to. Any comments or suggestions can be sent by email to customerservice@enslow.com.

Portions of this book originally appeared in the book *BMX Racers* by Ellen C. Labrecque.

**Photo Credits:** Cover, pp. 29, 31 Sergei Bachlakov/Shutterstock.com; p. 1 Michael Woodruff/Shutterstock.com; pp. 4, 7 Carl De Souza/AFP/Getty Images; pp. 5, 32 Harry How/Getty Images; pp. 9, 10, 12, 14 homydesign/Shutterstock.com; pp. 15, 36, 41 Icon Sportswire/Getty Images; p. 19 Getty Images; p. 21 Rick Kern/WireImage/Getty Images; pp. 23, 26 Rodger Bosch/AFP/Getty Images; p. 24 Digital Light Source/Universal Images Group/Getty Images; p. 28 Jamie Squire/Getty Images; p. 35 Joe Scarnici/Getty Images; p. 39 Modfos/Shutterstock.com.

# Contents

# 1 Let the BMXing Begin!

It was the 2016 Summer X Games in Austin, Texas, and the crowd was ready for a show. BMX street rider Garrett Reynolds had already dominated the event in the past, earning seven of the eight golds ever given for street BMX. Would he rule once again?

"Of course I want to win," Reynolds said. "BMX Street at X Games has obviously been the biggest thing to happen to my career." He continued, "In street, it's all super technical tricks and almost impossible combinations, and if any one of these guys puts all their tricks together, they could win, while any one of us could just

Garrett Reynolds has ruled the BMX street competition at the X Games, winning gold almost every time.

as easily fall during our runs. Everyone shines in their own way, and there are so many styles and types of riding to appreciate that it could also just be up to the judges on the day."

For fifty seconds, eyes were glued to the talented Reynolds as he performed his jumps, spins, and tricks. Announcers followed his every move as he nailed each maneuver. But when he landed an impressive 540-degree spin, down a staircase, the excitement grew. By the end of his run, the ESPN announcer exclaimed, "I'm gonna make the call that we have a gold medalist ... As soon as the pressure is on, he rides amazing." And the announcer was right. Reynolds won gold.

## What a Feeling

What's it like to drop down the sloped starting ramp at a BMX race? "Imagine riding straight down the side of a three-story building," said Mike King, former director of the US Olympic BMX program. When the gate drops, eight BMX riders take off down the 26-foot (8-meter) starting ramp. When they get to the bottom of the ramp, they've hit speeds of about 40 miles (63 kilometers) per hour!

Riders of bicycle motocross, better known as BMX, take big jumps and sharp turns. BMX races take place on dirt tracks. Pro riders have said participating in a BMX race is like riding a roller coaster.

Usually, eight riders compete in each heat, or moto. A BMX event begins with qualifying rounds. Successful riders move on to quarterfinals, semifinals, and finals.

## A Historic Day

For the first time in Olympic history, BMX cycling is on the event list. It is August 22, 2008—the day of the men's and women's gold medal BMX races at the Olympic Games in Beijing, China—and BMX is making its Olympic debut. All the riders are wearing shielded helmets and brightly colored padded suits. They are about to make history.

At the Olympic debut of BMX racing, Maris Strombergs (*right*) and Mike Day (*center*) compete during the men's finals at the 2008 Beijing Olympic Games.

## 2016 Olympic Medals for USA

"I can't describe how great this feels. It's a moment I've been dreaming of since I was sixteen," said Connor Fields. The Las Vegas native was thrilled to be crowned men's BMX champion at Rio 2016 and bring home gold for the USA. "To finally hear the words 'Olympic champion' after my name is like a dream."

Alise "the Beast" Post, who started racing when she was six years old, brought home the silver medal for Team USA. She had the best finish by an American woman in Olympic BMX history. By the first turn, the men's race is already decided. Maris Strombergs of Latvia leads the whole time. He zooms across the finish line for first place. Mike Day and Donny Robinson of the United States win the silver and bronze medals.

In the women's race, two French riders, Anne-Caroline Chausson and Laetitia le Corguille, take gold and silver. Jill Kintner of the United States wins bronze.

"We put on a great show," said Robinson, "and showed everyone that the sport is really awesome."

# 2 The Beginning of BMX

BMX racing began in Southern California in the late 1970s. Here's the story. In the early 1960s, motorcycle racing was very popular in the United States. Schwinn, a bicycle company, created a model called the Sting-Ray in 1963. The Sting-Ray was supposed to feel like a motorcycle. It had 20-inch (51-centimeter) wheels, which were smaller than the wheels of other bikes. This allowed kids to turn the bike easily and to do wheelies and other simple tricks.

In 1971, a motorcycle documentary called *On Any Sunday* was released. Kids watched all of their favorite motorcycles racers in

BMX racing is more popular now than it was when it burst onto the scene as a new sport in the 1970s.

action, and they began to copy the moves on their bicycles. In 1974, the first national BMX race was held. It was called the Yamaha Gold Cup, and it took place in Van Nuys, California. BMX racing was on its way!

## Tricks and Spins

By the mid-1970s, BMX riders were taking their new sport in different directions. Some kids in Southern California started riding in empty swimming pools. Other riders were pulling tricks in new skate parks.

In October 1975, the magazine *BMX Weekly* showed a picture of racer Stu Thomsen doing a 360-degree midair spin on his bike. Kids started trying Thomsen's trick. Soon, BMX riders were going freestyle.

Freestyle BMX is when riders pull tricks on their bikes. The sport is divided into five main categories: vert, street, park, dirt, and flatland. Vert riders do tricks on ramps and in empty pools. Street riders do tricks on the street. Park riders do their stuff on ramps in skate parks. Dirt riders cruise over dirt jumps. Flatland riders perform on any hard surface, such as a driveway.

## BMXers by the Numbers

Today, there are about seventy-five thousand American BMX racers. Their ages range from four to seventy-five. Racers compete on more than three hundred sanctioned tracks in the United States and Canada. The sport has four ability levels: novice (beginner), intermediate, expert, and pro. The season runs all year long, from January to December.

Two organizations used to run BMX races in the United States: the National Bicycle League (NBL) and the American Bicycle Association (ABA). In 2011, the ABA merged with the NBL and now operates as a single organization: USA BMX. The organization works closely with USA Cycling, a nationwide organization for all cycling sports.

Freestyle BMX is a way for riders to show off their acrobatic skills on a bike. Tricks, spins, and jumps are all part of the act.

## BMX Timeline

**1963** Schwinn creates the Sting-Ray, the first BMX bike.

**1971** The motorcycle movie *On Any Sunday* is released in the United States.

**1974** The first national BMX race is held. *Bicycle Motocross News*, the first national magazine to cover BMX racing, publishes its first issue.

**1984** The American Freestyle Association is formed, and freestyle BMX becomes an official sport.

**1995** The first X Games (then called the Extreme Games) take place in Providence, Rhode Island.

**1996** Freestyler Mat Hoffman wins his tenth vert freestyle world championship in ten years.

**2001** Soaring 50 feet (15.24 m) into the air, Hoffman sets a world record for height on a bike.

**2005** *Joe Kid on a Sting-Ray* is released. This documentary tells the story of BMX.

**2008** BMX makes its Olympic debut at the Summer Games in Beijing, China.

**2011** The ABA merges with the NBL and begins operating as a single organization: USA BMX.

**2016** Connor Fields takes home gold and Alise Post earns silver for Team USA at the Olympic Games in Rio de Janeiro, Brazil.

# BMX Basics: The Bike

3

It may be quite obvious, but the first thing you need to do before you start racing is to find the right BMX bike for you. You can use most bicycles with 20- to 24-inch (51- to 61-cm) wheels. A 20-inch (51 cm) is a standard BMX bike. Anything larger than a 24-inch (61-cm) bike is known as a cruiser. BMXers don't use equipment that sticks out, such as kickstands, chain guards, and reflectors. You should also decide what you want to do on your bike. There are four kinds of BMX bikes: racing, dirt jumping, freestyle (vert, street, and park), and flatland. If you want to race, use a bike that is lightweight and easy to pedal fast. If you plan to

Make sure you ask an expert to help you find the right sized bike for you. When you feel comfortable on your bike, you will have an easier time mastering your skills.

do dirt jumping or freestyle moves, get a heavier bike. The stronger the bike, the better it will handle all the tricks you pull.

## Bike Fit and Price

Next, decide how big the bike should be. Ask the experts at the bike store for help. They'll be able to find the right fit for you. Most BMX frames are 19 to 22 inches (48 to 56 cm) long. Picking out a bike is like trying on new pants. You may have to "try on" a few bikes until you find just the right one.

New BMX bikes can be expensive. You can find great deals on used bikes on the internet. Also, most bike stores sell used bikes or last year's models at reasonable prices.

## Bike Guide

*Ride BMX* has come up with a list of tips for buying a BMX bike:

1. Know your intentions. Once you know how you want to use your bike, you can narrow down your options.
2. Look for chromoly, a type of strong, lightweight metal alloy in high-end BMX bike frames. If you have narrowed down your choice to two bikes, and one uses the alloy, choose that one.
3. Pick the proper size. Test the bike in a parking lot before you buy it so that you know that size fits you well.
4. Don't expect things to last forever. Learn to work on your bike and know that some parts will need replacing.
5. Small parts make a big difference. Check out all the bike's components to see what kind of quality you are buying. Name brand parts, such as Odyssey or SNAFU, are better quality than generic parts. Also check to see whether the sprocket size is outdated or unnecessarily large.

6. Know how much money you can spend. Set your budget and stick to it. Once you know what you want to buy comparison shop online or with other competitive shops.
7. Look at the weight. A light bike usually has quality, stronger parts on it. A lighter bike may be easier to control and less tiring to ride.
8. Don't get sold on gimmicks or colors. You can always paint your frame to make it more your style.
9. Look for a shop service plan. Many shops give you a free service plan when you buy a complete bike. Bring your bike in for maintenance and a tune-up to keep it running smoothly and safely. You might even learn some tips for working on your bike yourself.
10. Build it up right. If you are building a complete bike that you ordered, be sure to have a knowledgeable friend or expert help you assemble it.
11. Look for sealed bearings in the wheels, bottom brackets, and headsets. They help your bike roll smoother for a longer time.

Greg Leasure, former track director of the ABA, offers these additional tips on how to shop for a bike:

1. Find a bike that is the right fit for you. Don't choose style over comfort.
2. Buy a bike that is already assembled. It's less expensive and safer than buying parts and putting them together yourself.
3. Don't spend money on accessories such as pegs and kickstands. They aren't allowed in races anyway.

## How Heavy Is a BMX Bike?

- BMX freestyle bike: 26 pounds (12 kilograms) and above
- BMX racing bike: 20 to 23 pounds (9 to 10 kg)
- Professional road-racing bike: 15 pounds (7 kg)

### Racing Bikes

A racing bike is best for dirt track racing and going fast for short distances off-road. Racing bikes don't have accessories such as kickstands, reflectors, or even front brakes. The less "stuff" on the bike, the safer it is to race and the faster you will go.

1. **Wheels**—The tires are extra knobby to provide a good grip on dirt tracks. The front tire has no brake—it is not necessary for racing. The wheels usually have thirty-two spokes.
2. **Frame**—Most racers like their bike as light as possible because it goes faster that way. The lighter the frame, the more expensive the bike will be. The lightest frames are made of aluminum, which does not rust.
3. **Pedals**—Sharp teeth on the pedals help provide the best grip.
4. **Seat**—The seat moves up and down so the bike can grow as you grow.
5. **Cranks and Chainwheels**—These parts send your "pedal power" to the wheels. The taller you are, the longer the crank arm will need to be.
6. **Brakes**—Racing bikes have only a rear brake. A pull grip on the handlebar gives you the best stopping power.

There are different styles of BMX bikes for the different types of riding. Once you decide on the type of riding you will do, you can narrow down your options.

## Dirt-Jumping Bikes

Dirt-jumping bikes are best for riding around town, jumping over dirt hills, and riding on trails.

1. **Wheels**—These tires have the heaviest treads of all BMX bikes. They provide the ultimate grip while jumping and landing on dirt hills. Like the racing bike, the front tire of a dirt jumper has no brake.
2. **Frame**—The frame should be sturdy to last through plenty of pounding from jumps.
3. **Brakes**—Dirt-jumping bikes have rear brakes called U-brakes. These brakes are a bit gentler than racing bike brakes, so that dirt jumpers can do certain tricks.
4. **Seat**—The seat is large and cushioned. This helps soften the blow on landings.

## Freestyle and Flatland Bikes

Freestyle and flatland bikes are almost the same. The main difference is that flatland bikes have smaller frames. Both types of bikes are used for doing highly technical tricks on smooth surfaces. Freestyle bikes are often used for pulling stunts in skate parks.

1. **Wheels**—The tires have fairly smooth treads. They are designed for pavement, which is easy to grip. Each wheel has two pegs. These are used for tricks.
2. **Handlebars**—The handlebars rise steeply to give riders more room for tricks. The front brake cable is usually run through a detangler or gyro.
3. **Gyro**—The gyro allows the handlebars to spin all the way around without tangling up the cable.

4. **Frame**—The frame is sturdy and thick. It needs to be durable enough for all kinds of tricks. Freestyle bikes are much heavier than racing bikes.

5. **Seat**—The seat is usually made of hard plastic. Riders often stand on their seats when pulling certain tricks.

6. **Front and rear brakes**—Unlike other BMX bikes, freestyle and flatland bikes have brakes on both tires. This helps the rider perform tricks that require immediate stops.

Kevin Peraza takes a practice run for the BMX dirt event during the X Games in Austin, Texas, on June 2, 2016. Peraza won gold with his lawn-dart front flip.

## New Heights at the X Games

At the 2016 X Games in Austin, Texas, fans were closer to the action than ever before, thanks to new Intel technology. Bikes in the dirt competition contained an Intel Curie-powered module. This technology tracks real-time data, such as jump distance, speed, height, and landing force. Live broadcasts of the event gave announcers new insight into the specs of a rider's performance.

Following a landing of a lawn-dart front flip, the play-by-play analyst exclaimed, "Did you see that?! ... I cannot wait to see the Intel technology stats on that one!" Immediately, fans knew Kevin Peraza had reached 14 feet, 11 inches (4.5 meters) during his remarkable flip. Just as impressive was his top speed of 23.9 miles (38.6 km) per hour! With a 47-point score, just three points short of perfect, Peraza won his first X Games gold medal.

The Intel module is just one example of how technology can enhance a sporting event and improve the way athletes train.

## BMX and STEM

You may already know that STEM stands for "science, technology, engineering, and math." USA BMX is now offering an after-school program that combines STEM with BMX bicycles. When BMX racing was included in the Olympic Games, the sport's popularity grew. This new youth program is half STEM education and half exercise. Students get a great educational lesson, a BMX bike, a helmet, and membership to USA BMX. It's a great way to combine a popular sport with physical fitness and learning.

4

# Time to Ride

Sometimes BMX riders just want to step outside, jump on their bikes, and go for a ride. There is no reason you can't do this. You just have to be smart about riding around town.

**On Side Streets**—Remember to obey all traffic signs and rules. Save your tricks and jumps for the track. Watch closely for people crossing the street or kids playing games.

**Backyards**—Are you looking for bumps and dirt? Try riding around your backyard (with an adult's approval, of course). You can even set up your own racetrack.

When you practice your BMX street tricks,
make sure to obey all local traffic rules.

**Skate Parks**—Skate parks are safe places for riders to practice tricks. However, many of them do not allow bikes. Before showing up on your bike, find out if your local skate park allows riders. Some parks have certain hours when only bikers are allowed.

**Trails**—Your local park probably has trails where you can take your bike off road. It can even be exciting to hit the trails after a big rainfall. Bikes and mud are a fun combination!

## The USA's Most Bike-Friendly Cities

Minneapolis, Minnesota
San Francisco, California
Portland, Oregon
Denver, Colorado
Boston, Massachusetts

*Source: Forbes.com*

### Get on Track

Are you ready to hit a track? Tracks can be anywhere from 900 to 1,200 feet (274 to 366 m) long. Usually, there are three turns and four straightaways. Go online to find a track near you. Check out the USA BMX website. Once you find the track, ask about special days for first-time riders to practice. Your first day at a BMX track should not be for a race.

One of the biggest and best tracks in the United States is in E. P. "Tom" Sawyer State Park in Louisville, Kentucky. It hosts the USA BMX Derby City Nationals every year on Labor Day weekend. The track is open for practicing when there isn't a race going on.

Most tracks, like the one in Kentucky, include the same features.

**Start Hill**: Usually about a 10-foot-long (3 m) sloped hill. Riders try to pick up the most speed here.

The first time you head to the track, go with an experienced friend or rider. They will help guide you and give you tips as you get started in the sport.

**Speed Jumps**: Rounded hills that riders can cruise or jump over. Riders try not to jump too high so they won't lose speed in the air.

**Sweeper**: A flat bend without a bank.

**Table Top**: A basic jump with a flat middle section.

**Berms**: Banked turns. Riders can wipe out on berms if they aren't careful.

**Rhythm Section**: A line of small jumps.

**Whoops**: Steep speed jumps set in pairs.

## Buddy System

When you take your first ride at a track, go with an experienced friend or a member of the track staff. Lots of kids learn from older friends or siblings. Eleven-year-old Kelsey Van Ogle of Auburn, Washington, learned to ride from her older brother, fifteen-year-old Lain. Kelsey started riding with straight power because of her brother's guidance.

## First Olympic Track

The BMX track built for the 2008 Olympics was the most challenging track ever designed at the time. In addition to the 26-foot (8-m) starting ramp, it had a 10-foot (3-m) dirt jump. On the men's course, riders took a 35-foot (11-m) jump over the women's course!

"When we first saw the track in China, it made our jaws drop because it was so much bigger than the regular Supercross tracks," said American rider Donny Robinson, who won a bronze medal at the 2008 games.

Not to be outdone, the US team built almost the exact same track for riders to train on at the US Olympic Training Center in Chula Vista, California. With the help of the best engineers in the world, the US track was built in three months. It cost about $450,000.

What's next for the Chula Vista BMX track? It will be there to help riders train for the 2020 Olympic track in Tokyo, Japan.

## Around the World

**BMX is popular with kids outside the United States, especially in Europe and Australia. The sport has also grown in South America. There are seventy-five national BMX federations worldwide.**

A BMX rider does tricks during the Extreme Sports Camp for Kids at Camp Woodward, Pennsylvania.

## Camp Woodward

Way out in the woods of central Pennsylvania is a BMX paradise. Actually, it is a paradise for most action sports. It is called Camp Woodward, and it has 80 acres (32 hectares) of ramps, street courses, dirt jumps, and bowl complexes for action sports athletes. It also has 175,000 square feet (16,258 sq m) of indoor facilities, so athletes can train there all year long. Camp Woodward also has locations in California and Colorado.

Camp Woodward isn't just for the pros. From June to August, Woodward hosts kids from ages seven to eighteen. They come from all over the country. Woodward even sets up foam pits for young campers. This allows BMX riders to try new tricks without getting injured.

"Woodward has boosted bike stunt so much," says Kevin Robinson, a professional BMX vert rider. "Pros come from all over the world to use this facility."

# 5 Staying Safe

BMX riding is a ton of fun. But all riders should understand that it can be dangerous. With a just a few pieces of equipment, you'll be as safe as possible. Be sure to wear your safety gear every single time you hop on your bike.

Your helmet is the most important part of your safety gear. Why? A lot of young riders find their head moves around quite a bit when they ride. Some young riders are known for their bobble-head style of racing!

For racing, helmets should have a full face guard. For freestyle riding, a skate helmet should protect you from injury—but advanced freestyle riders use helmets with face guards as well. Make sure your helmet is approved by the US Consumer Product Safety Commission (CPSC).

Pro cyclists recommend spending the extra money on a certified helmet. This is not an area where you want to save money.

## Pads, Gloves, and Shoes

Both racers and freestylers wear a basic set of skate pads that cover their knees and elbows. Don't be fooled by pro freestylers who look like they aren't wearing pads. Their style is to wear the pads underneath their pants. Many top pros wear shin and ankle guards as well.

Most BMX riders wear gloves. Biking gloves help prevent blisters and make sure your hands don't slip off the handlebars. Your biking gloves should fit tightly.

BMXers must wear closed-toe shoes. Make sure the bottoms have good treads on them so they don't slip off the pedals.

## Be Safe and Smart on Your Bike

Wearing the right equipment is only part of being a safe BMXer. You also need to ride safely. Remember, don't ride above your ability level—especially in freestyle. Start with the easier tricks. It takes a long time and a lot of practice to perform the hard tricks successfully.

Stay aware of your surroundings as well as other riders. While racing, don't try to dart through the pack when there isn't a big enough opening. If you're riding in a skate park, make sure all ramps are clear before you take off.

Be smart about where you ride. Do not perform tricks in parking lots and on the street. These are dangerous and unacceptable places to ride. And remember, always wear your safety gear, especially your helmet.

"I've had a lot of injuries that could have been prevented if I'd been wearing safety gear," said former BMX freestyler Dave Mirra. "Now, I feel naked without [my gear]."

A proper racing helmet is the most important piece of safety gear you can wear. Protect your head from impacts and injuries so that you do not suffer from major injuries if you fall.

## The Dangers of Head Trauma

Dave Mirra, former BMX freestyler and winner of twenty-four X Games medals, suffered many concussions during his years of competition as well as a fractured skull in a car accident. When he retired from cycling, he started boxing as a hobby. After his death in 2016, he became the first action athlete to be diagnosed with chronic traumatic encephalopathy (CTE). This is a degenerative disease that can be found in the brains of people who have had multiple concussions or head impacts. Symptoms include headaches and dizziness, and it can lead to depression and suicide. Sadly, Mirra took his own life in 2016.

Dave Mirra finished first with this no hander in the vert competition of the 2004 X Games. Mirra was a memorable and popular pro BMX rider.

In the mid-1990s, Dave Mirra and pro BMX rider Ryan Nyquist were designing BMX bikes, and they were popular worldwide. During the X Games a few years later, Dave Mirra's signature Haro bicycle was front and center on every viewer's television screen. The Haro bike was hot and in demand.

After being a part of the Haro team through the end of 2006, Mirra started his own brand, Mirraco. But he accomplished most of his memorable feats on a Haro bike. That's how fans remember him. So, in Dave Mirra's honor, Haro released the 2017 tribute Dave Mirra bike. A majority of the earnings from the sale of this bike will be given to his family. Haro wants to honor Mirra's life and legacy. They remember the contribution he made to the world of BMX racing.

## Do a Bike Check

**Before every ride, do a quick bike check. Make sure of these things:**

- Your brakes are working
- All bolts and screws are tight
- Your seat is secure
- Your tires have the right amount of air

## Star Riders

If you are looking for some pros and fellow kid riders to look up to, here are just a few of the big names in USA BMX.

### BROOKE CRAIN

Visalia, California

Crain started riding at six years old after her family bought her a bike so that she would not feel left out when the family went to the track to watch her brother, Brandon, race. After graduating from high school in 2011, Crain focused on BMX racing full-time. She competed in the 2012 London Olympics and was the number one ranked USA BMX women's pro rider in 2017.

### CONNOR FIELDS

Las Vegas, Nevada

Fields began riding when he was seven, and after graduating high school, he finished on the podium at three consecutive world cup competitions. His 2012 national championship was topped by world championship wins in 2012 and 2013. But the icing on the cake was his gold medal win at the 2016 Rio Olympics.

### ALISE POST

St. Cloud, Minnesota

After her brother suggested she try it, Post started BMX racing when she was six years old. Born in 1991, Post backed out of her first race at the last minute. Less than twenty years later, though, she earned an Olympic silver medal. Post is nicknamed "the Beast." Post won the 2016 Olympic silver medal in Rio.

### GARRETT REYNOLDS

Toms River, New Jersey

A BMX street and park rider, Reynolds was born in the summer of 1990. By the time he was fifteen, he was having some great results in the X Games. Since he was eighteen, he has ruled the BMX street contest and Dew Tour events each year. He won gold again at the 2016 X Games in Austin, Texas, for his performance of street BMX riding.

Connor Fields and Alise Post won medals for Team USA at the 2016 Olympic Games in Brazil.

# Racing Your BMX Bike

## 6

Are you ready to race? Sign up for a USA BMX membership. (This usually costs about $60 a year.) The membership lets you participate in races and practice on the organization's tracks. You will also receive a number plate for your bike and a membership license for you to use when you register for events.

## Time for Strategy

Once you've mastered the basics of BMX, it's time to develop a racing strategy. The first rule is simple: practice, practice, practice! Try to hit as many different tracks as possible. The more hills and jumps you ride, the better you'll become. Also, invite friends along when you ride. The more riders, the more fun!

Some kid riders even train with the pros. For example, Vaughn Herrick, who is known for his fearless style, won the 2008 national championship in his age division when he was ten. Vaughn had practiced with US Olympian Kyle Bennett. They are both from the same hometown—Conroe, Texas.

## Starts and Turns

Once you are comfortable on the track, learn to balance at the starting gate with both feet on the pedals. This gives you a much faster start. Then go as fast as you can out of the gate and try to get the holeshot, or first position. This puts you ahead of the pack and helps you avoid getting in a tangle with other bikers.

Once you are in front, hold your position. Don't try to hit other riders, but don't let them knock you around either. When you hit jumps, stay low. Remember, it is called BMX racing. You're going for speed, not for major air.

Finally, try to stay on the outside of other riders on turns. On the outside line, you can see what everybody else is doing. This puts you in charge of the race. Keep pedaling all the way through the finish line. Many riders slow down, only to have another rider pass them for the win!

## Freestyle Tricks

If you prefer freestyle to racing, here are some tricks to try. Remember, always wear safety equipment. And don't try any trick unless you feel completely comfortable. Know your limits.

### BUNNY HOP

This is an aerial move on a bike. A lot of riders do bunny hops over curbs. You roll forward, lean back, and pull up on the handlebars. Next, lift your knees to help the back wheel lift off the ground. Once in the air, level the tires so you come back down evenly.

### BAR SPIN

Practice a bar spin on the ground first. You should start with your left hand backward on the grip and your right hand forward. While riding along, spin the handlebars clockwise 180 degrees. Once you have mastered this, try spinning the handlebars 360 degrees (all the way around) on flat ground.

### CAN CAN

You need to get some air to do this trick. Launch yourself off a ramp and kick your left or right foot over to the opposite side of the bike. The other foot stays on the pedal.

A more advanced trick is the no-footed can can. In this trick, you remove both feet from the pedals.

## X Games Best Trick

In 2016, the X Games added a new event: the Dave Mirra BMX Park Best Trick competition. The contest is in honor of late BMX legend Dave Mirra. The first winner was Kyle Baldock, nailing his 720 Double Tailwhip.

"Kyle Baldock is on fire!" the announcer roared. "It was the 720 Double Whip, right out of the gate pretty much, that gets him the win here."

A new tradition had begun.

You will get a faster start if you learn to balance with both feet on the pedals at the start of your race.

## It's the Day of the Race!

Race day at the track feels like a big party. Families and friends are there to cheer on the riders. Fans set up picnics and tents around the track. Music blares from the loudspeakers. Volunteers and staff members are also milling around. They will help answer any questions you might have.

On race day, arrive early so you can register and take some practice runs. Once you have finished practicing, check out the moto board. On the board you'll find your race number and gate lane for each race. Write these numbers down on your hand or a piece of paper.

Pay attention to the announcer on the loudspeaker. The announcer will tell you when your race is coming up. Right before the race, officials will check out your bike to make sure it is safe. Once it is race time, relax and have fun. Listen for the shouting and clapping as you come around the turns. Your family and friends will all be cheering for you!

### Family Fun

What's the best part of BMX? The races? The tricks? The dirt? All these things are fabulous. But what makes BMX truly special is that it is a family affair. Nobody is left on the sidelines! After all, a racer's age can be anywhere from four to seventy-five.

"Mom and dad are yelling at their kid to pedal," said Greg Leasure of the ABA. "Then, the kid can turn it around and yell at his mom or dad to pedal harder too."

## BMX Lingo

Every sport seems to have its own set of unique terms, used by athletes and fans alike. Here are some terms to learn if you are starting to take an interest in BMX racing.

brain bucket—a helmet
kicker—a jump ramp
potato chip—a bent bicycle wheel
Superman—a trick where a rider poses in a flying motion during a jump

BMX racers, like these who competed in USA BMX's Mile High Nationals in Colorado, are cheered on by family, friends, and fans.

With all this yelling and cheering, BMX races are loud. Gates crash with a bang, the announcers chatter nonstop, and music blares from the loudspeakers. All this noise only adds to the fun!

Many times, families plan their vacations around the biggest BMX races of the year. They travel with campers and tents and stay at or near the racetracks. Families pack plenty of food to make sure that everybody stays fueled throughout the day.

# Glossary

**accessories** Extra parts that go with something. For example, a kickstand is an extra part that comes with a bike.

**aerial** Happening in midair.

**assembled** Put together, with all parts in place.

**cruiser bicycles** Standard bicycles sold in most bike or toy stores. They usually have heavy-duty frames and at least a 24-inch (61-cm) wheel.

**debut** A first public appearance.

**documentary** A movie about real people, places, and events.

**federations** Groups of smaller organizations with a similar purpose.

**frame** The main part of a bike that connects the wheels and all other parts.

**gyro (detangler)** A bike part that allows the handlebars to spin all the way around without tangling up the brake cable.

**holeshot** The first rider out of the starting gate.

**intermediate** A person who is fairly good at something; neither a beginner nor an expert.

**moto** A heat, or round of a race, at a BMX event.

**pegs** Parts of a freestyle bike that screw on where the tire is mounted to the frame. They are the size and shape of a roll of quarters. They can be screwed onto the back or front wheel. Pegs are used for tricks.

**pull** To do a trick.

**skate parks** Parks built for skateboarders, inline skaters, and BMX bikers to ride and develop their technique. The parks are filled with ramps and jumps.

**straightaways** Long, straight sections of a track or road.

**top tube** The part of a bicycle frame that stretches across the top of the bike from the seat to the back wheel.

**treads** The parts of a bicycle tire that grip the road.

**vert** An extreme sport held on a U-shaped ramp that allows athletes to move up and down (vertically).

# Further Reading

## Books


Adamson, Thomas K. *BMX Racing.* Minneapolis, MN: Bellweather Media, 2016.

Lakin, Patricia. *Bicycles*. New York, NY: Aladdin, 2017.

Loh-Hagan, Virginia. *Extreme BMX Freestyle*. Ann Arbor, MI: Cherry Lake Publishing, 2016.

Maddox Jake. *BMX Bravery.* North Mankato, MN: Stone Arch Books, 2016.


## Websites

### CAMP WOODWARD

*campwoodward.com*

Read all about the action sports camp.

### OLYMPIC GAMES

*olympic.org/cycling-bmx*

The official site of cycling BMX in the Olympic Games.

### USA BMX

*usabmx.com*

Visit the site of USA BMX, which coordinates the national, regional, state, and local scheduling for all tracks as well as manages the US Olympic BMX trials.

# Index